LOOK INTO SPACE

EXPLORING SPACE

Jon Kirkwood

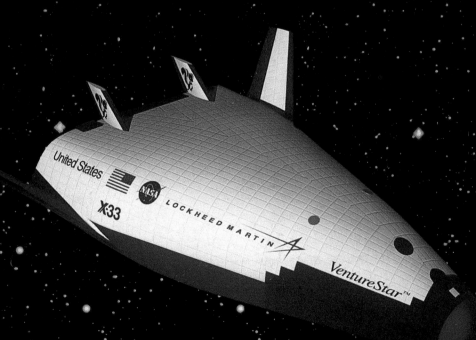

United States
NASA
X·33
LOCKHEED MARTIN
VentureStar™

ALADDIN/WATTS
LONDON • SYDNEY

An Aladdin Book
© Aladdin Books Ltd 1999
Produced by
Aladdin Books Ltd
28 Percy Street
London W1P 0LD

First published in Great Britain
in 1999 by
Franklin Watts Books
96 Leonard Street
London EC2A 4XD

ISBN 0-7496-3397-2

Editor: Jon Richards

Design

David West • CHILDREN'S BOOK DESIGN

Designer: Simon Morse

Illustrator: Ian Thompson

Picture research:
Carlotta Cooper/Brooks Krikler Research

Printed in Belgium

The author, Jon Kirkwood, is a freelance
author and editor who has written a
number of books for both adults and
children, mainly on astronomy.

CONTENTS

INTRODUCTION

Have you ever wondered what lies in space, beyond the comfort of the Earth? *Exploring Space* shows how humans have investigated the Universe, using telescopes, robot probes and by going there themselves – all from the comfort of your armchair. The book begins by showing what space exploration you can achieve from the Earth's surface, and goes on to recount our first steps beyond the Earth's atmosphere, out into the Solar System, and culminates in predictions about how we may reach the stars.

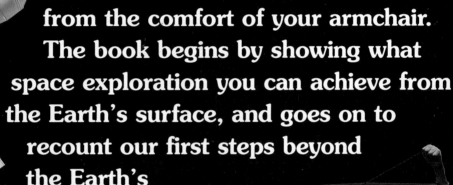

EXCELLENT EXPERIMENTS

Wherever you see this symbol (*below*), you'll find an experiment that you can do. Just follow the easy-to-understand instructions, and the results will open your eyes to the wonders of space. Find out how rockets work and how a space station could make its own artificial gravity.

LOOK UP!

You don't need a huge rocket to start exploring space, or even a large telescope. Just look up at the night sky and, if it's clear and the sky is dark, you can see a range of objects, including the Moon, some of the planets and thousands of stars. These offer a superb start to your own exploration of space.

LINE UP

Every so often, some of the moving objects in the sky appear to get close to each other. These include the Moon and the other planets. Here (*above*), the Moon, Venus and Jupiter all appear in the same part of the sky. The Moon is the crescent-shaped object in the lower left portion of the sky.

HELPING YOUR EYES

With a pair of good binoculars (*right*), you will be able to see far more stars in the sky than just with your eyes (*left*). You do not want a pair of high-magnification binoculars to look at stars. A magnification of seven times is good enough to see far more detail.

USING THE SKY

Before astronomers had telescopes, they used quadrants to measure the height of stars in degrees above the horizon. Another device that early astronomers used to help them observe stars was the astrolabe (*below*). This measured the positions of the Sun and bright stars in the sky. It was also used to help in navigation.

HOME-MADE QUADRANT

Make your own quadrant which will help you map the night sky. Ask an adult to cut out a quarter-circle shape from some stiff card. Using a protractor and a ruler, mark the degrees on the card's curved edge (*right*).

Now tie some string onto a lump of modelling clay. Then fix the other end of the string to the right angle of your quarter-circle (*left*). Attach two small pieces of card to the upper side of your quadrant to act as viewfinders. To observe the stars and find out their elevation above the horizon, line up a star in the viewfinders. Then read off the angle at which the length of string crosses the edge of the quadrant (*right*).

DIRTY LIGHT?

Have you ever wondered why it's harder to see stars above a city than above the countryside? The problem partly lies with 'light pollution'. Artificial light from streetlights, houses, factories and offices brightens the night sky above a city (*right*). This effectively 'drowns out' the light from fainter astronomical objects, making them almost impossible to see, even with a telescope. Because of this, astronomers need to observe stars far away from any towns and the light pollution they cause.

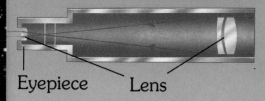

Eyepiece   Lens

REFRACTING TELESCOPE

In a refracting telescope, light is gathered and bent, or refracted, by a lens at one end of the telescope and brought to a focus at the other end (*above*). The image is seen through the lens in the eyepiece at the rear of the telescope, which also magnifies the image (*right* – in this case, a prism is bending light at a right angle to the tube so that it can be viewed comfortably).

REFLECTING TELESCOPE

In a reflecting telescope, light is gathered by a curved mirror at the back of the telescope (*left*). In a Newtonian telescope, the light is reflected back up the tube, off a second mirror and into the eyepiece. The image is viewed through the eyepiece on the side of the telescope (*right*).

Mirror

Eyepiece

Curved mirror

SCOPE FOR AMATEURS

To carry out a more detailed study of the night sky, you will need a telescope. As an amateur, you can use many types of telescope, such as refractors, reflectors and catadioptric telescopes – you can even build your own observatory!

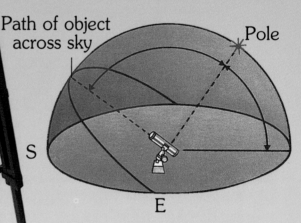

Path of object across sky   Pole

S   N

E

EQUATORIAL MOUNTING

A good, solid mounting is essential for a telescope used for astronomy. It will give a shake-free image. One commonly used type of mounting is called the equatorial mounting. With this type, one of the two axes of the mount points toward the pole. The telescope can then easily track an object across the sky as the Earth rotates on its axis (*above*).

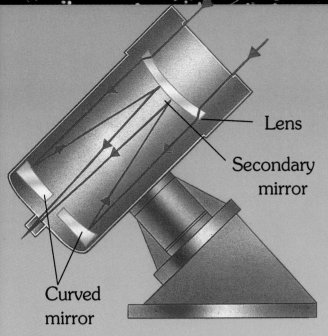

Lens

Secondary mirror

Curved mirror

CATADIOPTRIC TELESCOPE

A catadioptric telescope combines elements of the refracting and the reflecting telescopes. In this type, light is gathered by a curved mirror at the back, like a reflecting telescope, but there is also a lens at the front, like a refracting telescope. The curved mirror reflects light up to a secondary mirror that sends it out of the tube, via a hole in the centre of the main mirror, to an eyepiece where it is magnified. The secondary mirror is usually mounted on the rear of the lens (*left*).

OBSERVATORY

It is not easy to move even medium-sized telescopes around because they can be very heavy. It is best, if you can, to keep a telescope permanently set up in an observatory. Here, it can be protected from the elements but brought into action quickly when the sky is clear. An amateur observatory can be anything from a shed with a sliding roof to a proper dome with a large slit in it (*right*). Domes need to rotate, so that different parts of the sky can be seen.

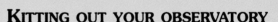

BENDING LIGHT

To get an idea of how a lens works, look through a magnifying glass at an object. As light rays from the object pass through the glass of the lens, they are bent, or refracted. The lens' shape means that they are bent in such a way as to make the image appear larger, or magnified.

KITTING OUT YOUR OBSERVATORY

Whether you build and equip your own observatory (*right*), or prefer to do something a little smaller, it is important to have the right basic equipment to look at the night sky. As well as a telescope or binoculars, you should also have a notebook to record your observations, a clock to make a note of the time, and a good sky map.

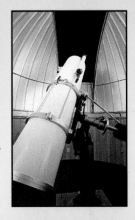

The Mauna Kea Observatory (*left*) is the highest observatory on Earth. It sits on top of a dormant volcano in Hawaii, 4,205 m (13,796 ft) above sea level. At this height, it is above a lot of the Earth's atmosphere. As a result, light and other radiation can reach it with less atmospheric interference than if the observatory were closer to sea level. There are a number of powerful telescopes that make use of the clearer viewing conditions at Mauna Kea.

GROUND-BASED ASTRONOMY

Professional astronomers use powerful telescopes to examine space. Some of these telescopes observe objects using visible light. However, other types of telescope can detect invisible parts of the spectrum, such as radio waves, while other devices detect mysterious particles, such as neutrinos.

MULTI-MIRRORS

The Keck II Telescope at Mauna Kea (*right*) is the world's largest optical telescope. Its main mirror measures 10 m (33 ft) across and is actually made up of 36 smaller hexagonal mirrors. Computers move these small mirrors to alter the focus and keep the image as clear as possible.

HALE TELESCOPE

One of the world's largest telescopes is the Hale Telescope at the Palomar Observatory in California (*above*). This is a reflecting telescope with a mirror 5 m (16.5 ft) across. The mirror, made of a type of glass called pyrex, weighs 14.5 tonnes and the tube for the telescope – an open structure of girders – is 18 m (60 ft) long.

NEUTRINO TANKS

Neutrinos are invisible particles which astronomers believe are given off by stars, like the Sun. These particles are difficult to detect – they can pass right through you without you noticing! To detect them, scientists have had to build fluid-filled tanks deep underground (*above*).

RADIO ARRAY

Astronomical radio telescopes pick up faint radio signals from objects in space. The large dishes focus radio waves onto a collector, from where the signals are sent to a computer for analysis. Astronomers can combine several dishes in a large array (*above*) to give a more detailed 'picture'.

ASTRONOMY THROUGH THE AGES

Throughout history, many people have looked up at the night sky and plotted the positions of the stars and planets. This ancient Chinese observatory (*below*) shows how complex these observations were. However, a revolution in astronomy occurred when the Italian astronomer and mathematician Galileo (*above*) turned one of the first telescopes upward in 1609. He saw moons orbiting Jupiter and features on the Moon. As equipment improved, so did the ability to discover new objects and test out theories. The first really large reflecting telescope was deployed by the German-born astronomer William Herschel in the late 18th century – it had a mirror about 1.2 m (4 ft) across (*left*).

With this instrument and others, he was able to see stars in some gas clouds, called nebulae. Refracting telescopes also advanced, and the largest ever made was one with a 1-m (3-ft) lens at the Yerkes Observatory in Wisconsin. This was installed in 1897 (*right*).

ROCKET POWER

Blasting clear of the Earth and reaching space requires a lot of power. The only engines that can deliver this power are rockets. There are two types of rocket: solid-fuel and liquid-fuel. They both work on the same principle. Fuel is burnt, creating hot gases which expand and push the rocket forwards.

EARLY ROCKETS

Although rockets date back to 11th-century China, the first liquid-fuel rocket was not launched until 1926, by Dr Robert Goddard (*left*). It flew to a height of just 12.5 m (41 ft)!

UP IN STAGES

The mighty Saturn V (*below*) which carried the Apollo spacecraft and astronauts to the Moon was, in fact, three rockets in one. When one stage was exhausted, it fell away and the next rocket stage started.

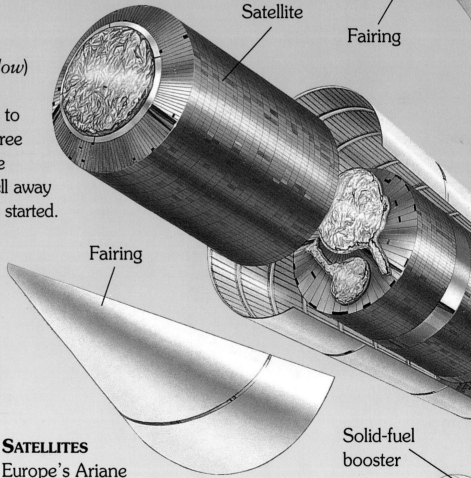

Satellite

Fairing

Fairing

Solid-fuel booster

SATELLITES

Europe's Ariane 5 rocket (*right*) can carry satellites weighing up to 20 tonnes into orbit around the Earth. The satellites sit on top of the rocket, protected by the fairing. When the rocket clears the Earth's atmosphere, the fairing falls away.

SHUTTLE LAUNCH

The 68-tonne Space Shuttle (*right*) is put into orbit by its own powerful liquid-fuel rocket motors and two solid-fuel boosters. The liquid fuel is carried inside the enormous orange fuel tank, which is strapped to the Shuttle's belly. When they've finished firing, the boosters are released and they parachute back to Earth where they are recovered for reuse. The fuel tank also falls away once it is empty.

ON MANOEUVRES

In space, the Shuttle is controlled by small manoeuvring rockets (*above*) which push it in different directions.

Liquid hydrogen tank

Liquid oxygen tank

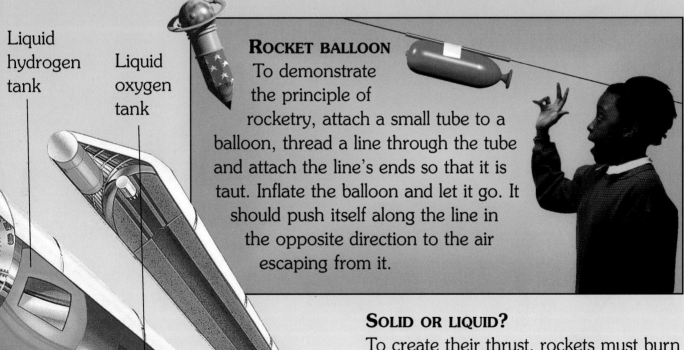

ROCKET BALLOON

To demonstrate the principle of rocketry, attach a small tube to a balloon, thread a line through the tube and attach the line's ends so that it is taut. Inflate the balloon and let it go. It should push itself along the line in the opposite direction to the air escaping from it.

SOLID OR LIQUID?

To create their thrust, rockets must burn their fuel with oxygen. Solid-fuel rockets burn their fuel with oxygen contained within the fuel. Liquid-fuel rockets carry their supply of oxygen in liquid form (*left*). Liquid-fuel rockets can be turned on and off as needed. Solid-fuel rockets burn until their fuel is used up.

TELESCOPES IN SPACE

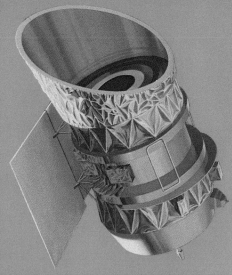

One of the advantages of going into space is that it offers a much better view of the Universe. Telescopes in orbit do not have their view disrupted by the atmosphere. They can also detect a whole range of invisible forms of radiation, such as x-rays. These cannot reach the Earth's surface because the atmosphere blocks them out.

INFRARED VISION

Infrared radiation is produced by hot objects, such as stars or regions of gas and dust around areas of star birth. To detect these regions clearly, scientists use satellites which orbit the Earth, such as IRAS (*above*).

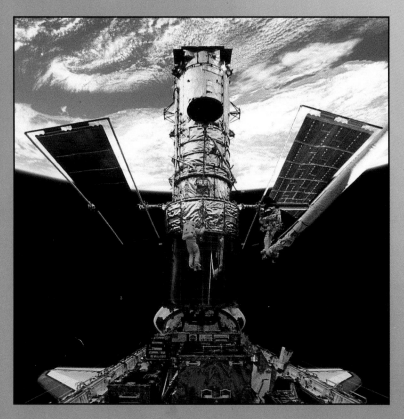

EYE IN THE SKY

The Hubble Space Telescope (HST – *left*) was launched in 1990. Above the distortion of the atmosphere, the HST can see further and more clearly than Earth-based telescopes. It can provide images which are ten times sharper than those produced on the ground. It is so sensitive that it could detect a coin at a distance of 640 km (400 miles)! As well as being a visual telescope, the HST is fitted with other types of sensors, including a high-resolution spectrograph and a high-speed photometer.

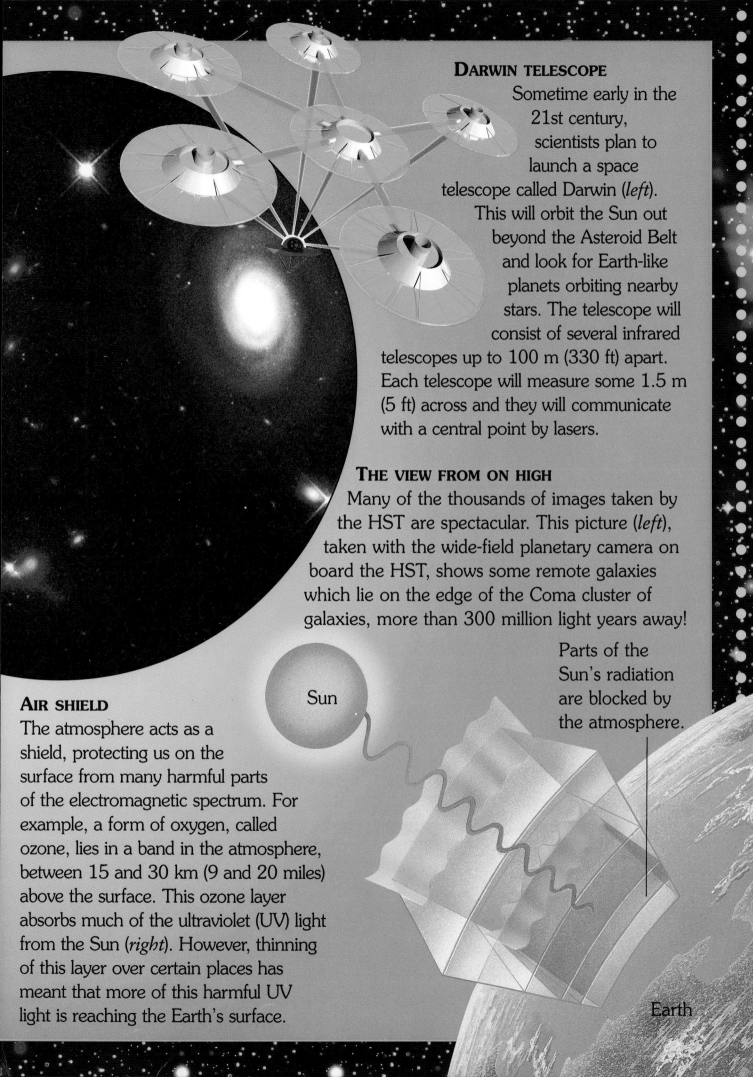

DARWIN TELESCOPE

Sometime early in the 21st century, scientists plan to launch a space telescope called Darwin (*left*). This will orbit the Sun out beyond the Asteroid Belt and look for Earth-like planets orbiting nearby stars. The telescope will consist of several infrared telescopes up to 100 m (330 ft) apart. Each telescope will measure some 1.5 m (5 ft) across and they will communicate with a central point by lasers.

THE VIEW FROM ON HIGH

Many of the thousands of images taken by the HST are spectacular. This picture (*left*), taken with the wide-field planetary camera on board the HST, shows some remote galaxies which lie on the edge of the Coma cluster of galaxies, more than 300 million light years away!

Parts of the Sun's radiation are blocked by the atmosphere.

Sun

AIR SHIELD

The atmosphere acts as a shield, protecting us on the surface from many harmful parts of the electromagnetic spectrum. For example, a form of oxygen, called ozone, lies in a band in the atmosphere, between 15 and 30 km (9 and 20 miles) above the surface. This ozone layer absorbs much of the ultraviolet (UV) light from the Sun (*right*). However, thinning of this layer over certain places has meant that more of this harmful UV light is reaching the Earth's surface.

Earth

SATELLITES

Not only does a position in orbit offer a good view of space, it also offers a good view of the Earth. Ever since the first satellite, Sputnik 1 (*left*), was launched in 1957, satellites have been used to reflect radio and television signals, examine the Earth's surface, spy on different countries and tell us exactly where we are. Since 1957, more than 5,000 satellites have been launched into Earth orbit, with hundreds more planned.

OVERHEAD, ALL THE TIME

Global Positioning System (GPS) satellites orbit at an altitude of 20,200 km (12,500 miles), going around the Earth once every 12 hours. With 24 satellites in orbit (*above*), this means that there are always three GPS satellites overhead.

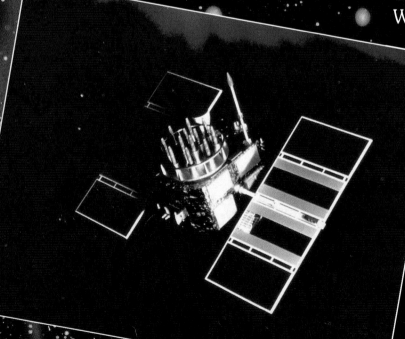

GLOBAL POSITIONING SYSTEM

With a complete system of 24 satellites, the Global Positioning System can tell a person his or her position to within 10 m (33 ft), and his or her altitude to the same accuracy. The system relies on at least three GPS satellites (*left*) giving a bearing to a handset held by the person. From where these three bearings cross, a computer can work out the latitude, longitude and altitude.

LOOKING DOWN ON US

The Landsat satellites (*right*), also known as the Earth Resources Technology Satellites (ERTS), are unmanned satellites that have been providing images and information about Earth's natural resources (*see below*) since the launch of Landsat 1 in 1972. The satellites are designed to take images of areas of the ground that are about 184 km (115 miles) square.

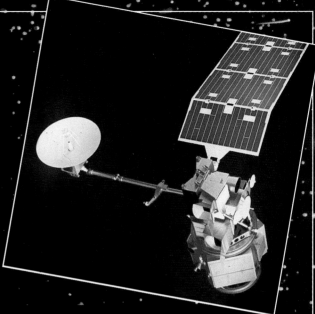

EXAMINING THE GROUND

Landsat satellites are fitted with cameras and other sensors to give scientists a detailed view of the ground. These satellites are used to collect information about the Earth's natural resources, such as the location of mineral deposits, the condition of farmland and forests, and to detect ecological changes. This information can be displayed as colour-coded photographs, such as this image of Los Angeles (*left*).

GETTING YOUR BEARINGS

You can work out where you are in a way not unlike that used by a GPS system. You need a map, a compass, a protractor, a ruler and a pencil. Look at an object that you can identify on the map, such as a building. Point your compass north and read off the angle which points towards the object. This is its bearing from your position. Now draw a line on the map which runs through the object at the same angle to north as the bearing you took (the top of the map is usually north). Repeat this for a different object. Where the two lines cross on the map is your location (*right*).

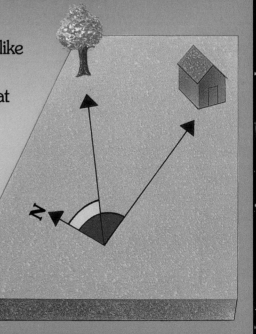

REACHING THE MOON

Since the early days of space exploration, the Moon has been the target for a great number of spacecraft. Some of these have even carried people, but the majority have been robot probes. These have told us a great deal about the Moon, even revealing the presence of frozen water in some of its darkest craters.

APOLLO
Between 1969 and 1972, the United States landed 12 men on the Moon as part of the Apollo space programme (*above*) – the last three missions even had their own Moon buggy!

FAR SIDE OF THE MOON
Launched on 4th October 1959, Luna 3 (*left*) became the first spacecraft to fly around the Moon. In doing so, it sent back images of the far side of the Moon, a side which, because of the Moon's spin and orbit, no one had ever seen before.

LUNA 16
Luna 16 (*right*) was a robot probe which reached the Moon in September 1970. It dug up samples of Moon rock and placed these inside a capsule on top of the craft. This capsule then blasted clear of the Moon and carried the samples back to Earth.

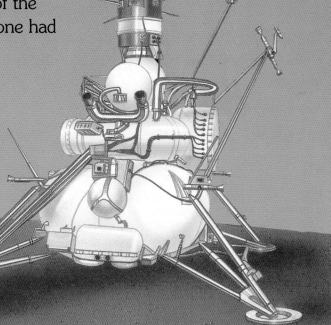

PROSPECTOR

When the Lunar Prospector (*right*) arrived at the Moon in September 1997, it was the first NASA mission to the Moon for some 25 years. From its orbit, 100 km (60 miles) above the Moon's surface, it had a range of tasks to perform, one of which was to see if there might be water on the Moon. It found huge quantities of water ice buried in the soil in craters at the lunar poles where the Sun never reaches to warm them up and evaporate the water.

RETURN TO THE MOON

The discovery of water on the Moon has increased speculation as to when people will return to its surface. A future lunar mission (*left*) may not have to carry all of its own water supply. It could also separate the Moon water into its basic atomic components. This would produce oxygen, which the astronauts could breathe, and hydrogen, which could be used as fuel for their spacecraft.

JAPANESE PROBES

Japan has plans for a number of probes to the Moon. These include the Selene project which will consist of an orbiting satellite and a lander. Other probes include Lunar-A. This will orbit the Moon some 250 km (150 miles) above its surface. From here it will fire three small probes into the Moon (*right*). These will dig into the surface and look for 'moonquakes' and any heat coming from the Moon's interior.

THE INNER PLANETS

Mercury and Venus, the innermost planets, are very difficult to observe from Earth. Mercury is very close to the Sun, whose glare stops us from seeing the planet clearly, while the surface of Venus is covered in thick clouds of swirling gas. The only details of these planets have been provided by probes.

MARINER 10

During the Mariner 10 (*below*) mission to Mercury, there were many problems with the craft. It had to make constant course corrections and its fuel supply ran low. To keep it on track, flight controllers used the probe's solar panels as sails to catch the solar wind and steer the spacecraft towards its final target.

THE SURFACE OF MERCURY

Mariner 10 made three close approaches to Mercury between 1974 and 1975. On its third approach it got to within 300 km (188 miles) of the planet. The probe returned pictures to Earth which showed that Mercury looked like the surface of our own Moon, being peppered with craters – big and small (*left*). The large craters are thought to be from impacts that happened a few hundred million years after the planet formed. Mercury also has flat plains and very long, high ridges, or scarps, running across it.

CLOSE-UP OF VENUS

The Russian probes Venera 9 and Venera 10 landed on Venus in 1975 (*right*). They survived their journey through the corrosive atmosphere of the planet and made a controlled soft landing before sending back black-and-white pictures from the planet's baking-hot surface.

THE FACE OF VENUS

Launched in 1989, NASA's Magellan spacecraft (*below*) was able to 'peer' through Venus' atmosphere and map the planet's surface by radar. From the data returned to Earth, computers were able to build up a map of the surface, including many detailed features (*above*).

VENERA TO VENUS

Russia sent a total of 11 Venera probes (*below*) to Venus. Venera 2, launched in 1965, flew to within 40,000 km (25,000 miles) of the planet in February 1966. In March 1966, by crash-landing on the surface, Venera 3 became the first probe to hit another planet. A total of seven Venera probes made soft landings on the planet's surface, sending back data about its harsh conditions. The last Venera, Venera 16, was launched in 1983.

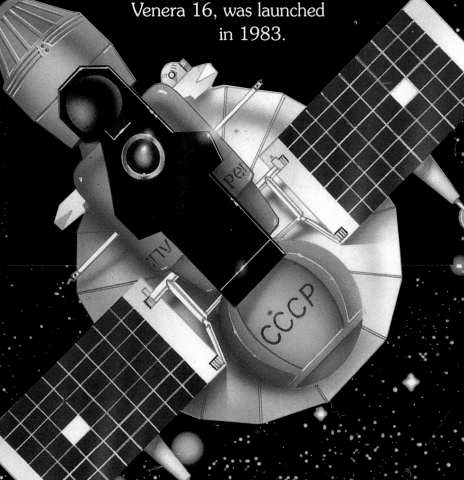

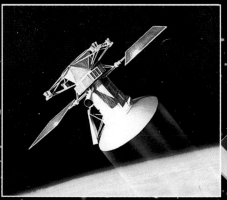

EXPLORING MARS

Even with the most powerful telescopes, very little detail can be seen of the Martian surface from Earth. However, visits by probes over the last 30 years have revealed a planet where liquid water once flowed and where polar ice-caps change size, just like the Earth's polar ice-caps. Soon the surface of Mars will be more accurately mapped than some parts of the Earth!

VIKINGS ON MARS
The two Viking missions, launched in 1975, each consisted of an orbiting satellite and a lander (*above*). The landers carried out experiments on the surface and sent the data back to Earth via the two orbiters.

THE PHONY FACE
Pictures taken during the Viking missions showed what seemed to be an image of a face on the Martian surface (*below*). This caused a lot of speculation back on Earth, and for many years some people believed that this 'face' was, in fact, a message from a Martian civilisation. However, more detailed images recently taken by another probe, the Mars Global Surveyor, showed the face to be nothing more than a bumpy hill (*above*).

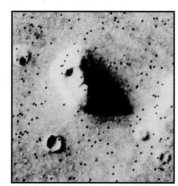

SOFT LANDING
To see how a parachute slows an object down, attach a lump of modelling clay to a large piece of cloth using thread, with one thread tied to each corner. Throw the modelling-clay and the cloth up in the air. As the modelling clay falls back to earth, the cloth opens. The large area of the cloth increases the air resistance, slowing the descent of the modelling clay.

SURVEYOR '98

Mars Surveyor '98 is a two-staged mission to Mars. The first stage is the Mars Climate Orbiter (*right*) which will orbit around the two poles. The second stage, launched a month after the orbiter, is the Mars Polar Lander. This will touch down on the surface near to Mars' south pole.

The two probes will study the Martian climate and measure the amount of water and gases in the polar ice-cap.

AIR BAGS

To save on fuel, Pathfinder was designed to slow its descent using parachutes and then bounce onto the surface, protected by air bags (*right*).

MARTIAN ROVER

Mars Pathfinder reached the Martian surface on 4th July 1997. Once it had deflated its air bags and unfurled its solar panels, the probe released a small roving vehicle called Sojourner. This took short trips across the surface to investigate rocks and other features (*right*).

THE OUTER PLANETS

Even though Jupiter, Saturn, Uranus and Neptune are the Solar System's largest planets, they are too distant to see in detail. Our only clear images of them have come from probes, such as Pioneers 10 and 11 and Voyagers 1 and 2, which crossed huge distances to visit them.

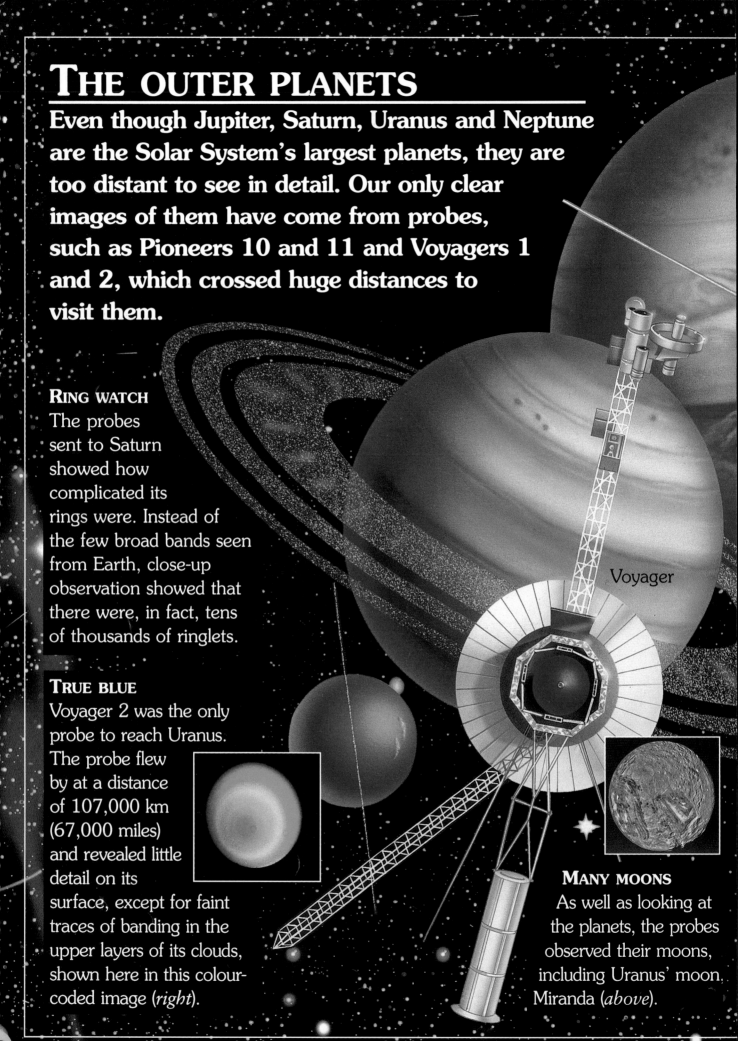

Voyager

RING WATCH

The probes sent to Saturn showed how complicated its rings were. Instead of the few broad bands seen from Earth, close-up observation showed that there were, in fact, tens of thousands of ringlets.

TRUE BLUE

Voyager 2 was the only probe to reach Uranus. The probe flew by at a distance of 107,000 km (67,000 miles) and revealed little detail on its surface, except for faint traces of banding in the upper layers of its clouds, shown here in this colour-coded image (*right*).

MANY MOONS

As well as looking at the planets, the probes observed their moons, including Uranus' moon, Miranda (*above*).

NEPTUNE'S RINGS

Voyager 2 was only able to take this view of the faint rings which surround Neptune (*right*) by blocking out the light reflected from the surface of the giant gas planet.

Pioneer

NEAR NEPTUNE

Voyager 2's images from Neptune revealed spots and storms on the planet's surface (*below*). Measurements taken by the probe showed that Neptune has the fastest winds of any object in the Solar System.

PATHS OF THE PROBES

In order to visit the giant planets, the Voyager and Pioneer probes used the so-called gravitational 'slingshot technique'. Here, each spacecraft flew close to a planet and used the planet's force of gravity to speed the spacecraft up. Voyager 2 used the gravity of all four of the giant planets to speed it up, before heading out of the Solar System and into deep space (*right*).

Pioneer 10

Voyager 2

Pioneer 11

Voyager 1

EXPLORING JUPITER

The Pioneer and Voyager probes (*see* pages 22-23) revealed Jupiter to be a fascinating planet with its own mini solar system of moons. Further investigation was needed, and another probe, Galileo (*right*),

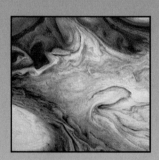

was sent. Scientists were so amazed by this probe's findings that its mission was extended.

CASUAL VISITORS

All four Pioneer and Voyager probes visited Jupiter (*see* pages 22-23). They sent back some amazing close-up images of the gassy giant, including this picture of the swirling gas clouds which make up Jupiter's cloud tops (*above*). These images also included this spectacular shot of Jupiter's rings, lit from behind by the Sun (*below*).

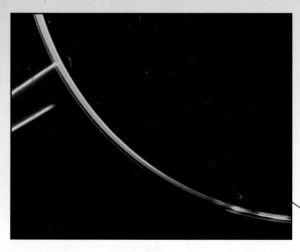

GALILEO

In 1995, Galileo became the first probe in over 16 years to visit Jupiter. Despite having a problem with its umbrella-like antenna, Galileo carried out its mission, examining the planet and many of its moons including Ganymede (*below right*), the largest moon in the Solar System. Galileo discovered that Ganymede is giving off hydrogen gas and that it is the only moon to have a magnetic field.

OTHER MOONS

Jupiter has at least 16 moons, ranging from Ganymede, the largest, to its smaller moons, including Amalthea, the closest moon to Jupiter (*left*). Among the larger moons, Galileo investigated Callisto (*below*) and found that it may have a liquid ocean beneath its icy, cratered crust. It also looked at Europa (*below*). Galileo found evidence to suggest that Europa, like Callisto, has a liquid ocean beneath its crust. This crust has huge cracks in its surface where new ice has formed.

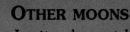

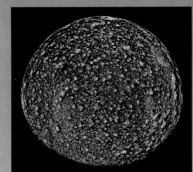

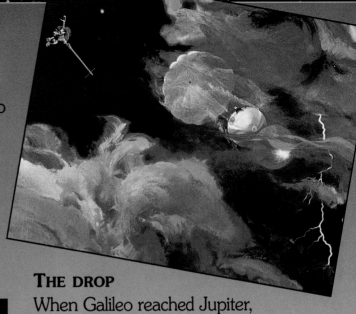

THE DROP

When Galileo reached Jupiter, it released a small probe into the planet (*above*). The probe fell into Jupiter for 57 minutes before it was crushed by the pressure of the atmosphere. As it fell, it measured temperature, pressure and the chemical make-up of the cloud layers.

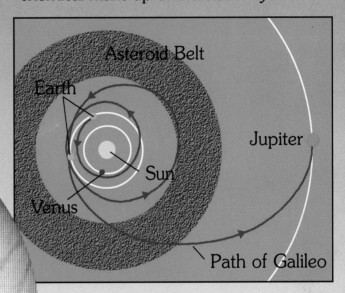

Asteroid Belt

Earth

Jupiter

Sun

Venus

Path of Galileo

TRAVELLING TO JUPITER

Galileo was launched by the Space Shuttle in 1989. Its six-year voyage used the gravity of Venus and Earth to 'slingshot' it further into space, thus saving on fuel (*above*). During its flight it had close encounters with two asteroids, Gaspra and Ida (*see* page 27). It arrived at Jupiter in 1995, and is still sending back information today.

OTHER BODIES

Not every probe has been sent to look at the planets. Our Solar System contains many other objects, including the Sun, asteroids and comets. Investigating these objects has proved difficult – asteroids are very small, comets throw out potentially dangerous particles and looking at the Sun can mean going where no other spacecraft has gone before!

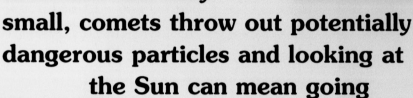

THE VOYAGE OF ULYSSES

In 1992, Ulysses (*left*) used the gravity of Jupiter to sling itself into an orbit around the Sun's poles. In doing so, it became the first spacecraft to leave the plane of the Solar System. The mission explored the Sun's corona, the solar wind and the Sun's magnetic field.

SOHO

The Solar and Heliospheric Observatory, or SOHO (*left*), was designed to study the Sun's insides, its atmosphere and the solar wind. It was placed in an orbit 1.5 million km (900,000 miles) in front of the Earth so that its view of the Sun was uninterrupted. Among many other things, it has discovered that solar flares cause quakes on the Sun's surface and that the Sun has tornados bigger and faster than any on Earth.

CLOSE TO COMETS

When Halley's Comet returned in 1986, no less than five probes were sent to observe it. They included the ESA's Giotto probe (*left*) and the Russian probe Vega. Giotto also went on to investigate Comet Grigg-Skjellerup in 1992.

GETTING A BEATING

To protect Giotto from the particles which the comet threw off to form its tail (*right*), it had a special shield made from aluminium and kevlar.

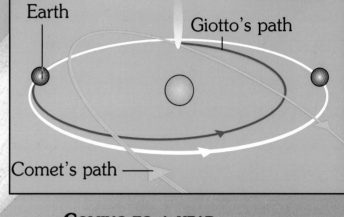

Earth

Giotto's path

Comet's path

COMING TO A HEAD

Giotto's flight path was accurately planned so that the probe passed to within 540 km (338 miles) of Halley's nucleus. After the spacecraft's launch on 2nd July 1985, it travelled for seven months before meeting the comet (*above*). Despite Giotto's protective shield, it was damaged by debris from the comet's head.

ROCK WATCHING

During Galileo's six-year flight to Jupiter (*see* pages 24-25), the probe passed through the Asteroid Belt twice, flying close to two asteroids, Ida and Gaspra. Galileo discovered that Ida has a moon of its own, another tiny asteroid named Dactyl (*above*). Dactyl orbits Ida at an average distance of just 90 km (56 miles).

GASPRA

On Galileo's first trip through the Asteroid Belt, it flew to within 5,300 km (3,300 miles) of the asteroid Gaspra (*left*). Gaspra is quite a small asteroid, and it measures 19 km (12 miles) by 12 km (7.5 miles).

HUMANS IN SPACE

Despite the success of robot probes, they are still unable to match the intelligence of a human. This is why it is important to have people in space. Here, they can launch new satellites (*right*), rescue old ones and build space stations. But getting into space is a risky business. In 1986, the Shuttle *Challenger* exploded, killing seven astronauts, and a recent collision between two Russian spacecraft nearly ended in disaster.

SATELLITE RESCUE

Even the most advanced satellite can go wrong. Rather than leave it broken, astronauts can capture the satellite (*above*) and bring it back to Earth for repair, or they can fix it in space. In 1993, astronauts were able to repair the Hubble Space Telescope (*see* pages 12-13) in space after a fault was detected.

CITIES IN THE SKY

Since the earliest days of space travel, people have built and maintained space stations. These have ranged from single-module stations, such as Salyut and Skylab, to larger, multi-module stations, such as the Mir station (*left*) and the International Space Station (*see* pages 30-31).

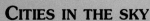

28

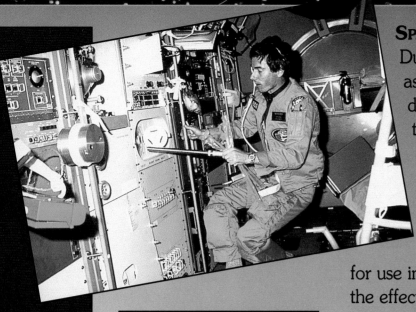

SPACE TO WORK IN

During their time in space, astronauts must work in quite difficult conditions. These include the confined room of a spacecraft and zero gravity (*left*). However, one of these difficult conditions – weightlessness – is vital to many experiments carried out in space. These include growing crystals for use in making medicines. On the Earth, the effects of gravity disrupt the growth of these crystals. In space, free from gravity, these crystals can grow unhindered.

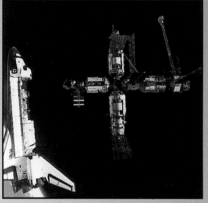

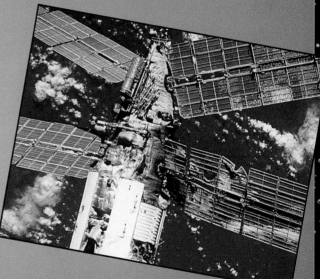

DOCKING IN SPACE

Linking two spacecraft in space is a difficult thing to do. In order to practise for the construction of the International Space Station, Space Shuttles have docked with the Mir station (*above*).

SPACE PROBLEMS

The dangers of living in space were highlighted on 25th June 1997. A Progress robot supply craft collided with the Mir Space Station, damaging solar panels (*above*) and causing the station to lose power. Mir was nearly abandoned, but extensive work by cosmonauts repaired the damage, allowing the station to continue its work.

WEIGHT TO GO

Before they go into space, astronauts train inside huge swimming pools which mimic zero-gravity conditions (*right*). The next time you go to a swimming pool, feel the gravity-defying effects of water by floating in it – only try this with adult supervision.

INTERNATIONAL SPACE STATION

On the 20th November 1998, the first part of the International Space Station (ISS) was launched. The ISS will consist of more than 100 parts, made by 16 different countries, and, when it is completed, it will be the largest space station ever built – even longer than a football pitch!

GETTING IT TOGETHER

All of the parts of the ISS will be built on Earth (*below left*). These parts will then be carried into orbit in 45 missions by the Space Shuttle and two types of Russian rocket. Here, astronauts will connect them all together.

STATION FACTS

When unfurled, the enormous solar panels (*above*), which will supply the station with power, will cover 2,508 sq m (22,144 sq ft). Once completed, the insides of the station will be as big as the space inside a jumbo jet, and it will have a 16-m (52-ft) robot arm to move objects into position.

MAKE WEIGHT

To see how the spin of a rotating space station can create artificial gravity, fill a small can with water, leave the lid off and tie it to some string. Spin it around your head and the force created by the rotation will keep the water in the can.

FUTURE STATION

Some time in the future, bigger space stations may be built in orbit around the Earth or other planets. One suggested design looks like a giant, spinning bicycle wheel (*above*). As this station slowly spins, the rotation creates a force which pushes the objects out from the centre. This creates artificial gravity for people living in the station's rim.

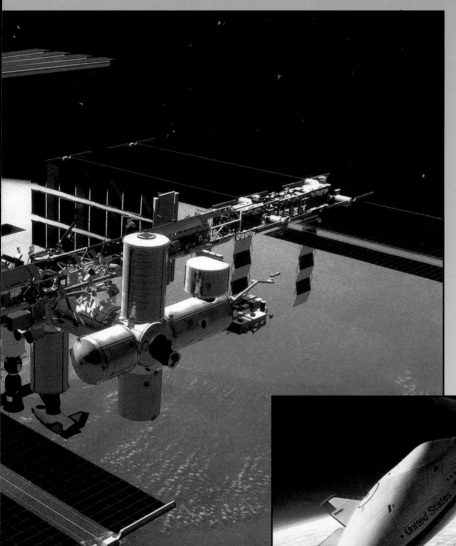

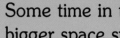

STATION LIFEBOAT

Should trouble arise on the ISS, astronauts may have to evacuate. Initially, they will use a Soyuz capsule to get down to Earth. This will be replaced by the X-38 (*left*). This will enter the atmosphere and then deploy a parasail to help steer it down to the ground.

EXPLOITING SPACE

Aside from the extraordinary scientific information which space has to offer, it can also provide us with our energy needs and financial wealth for the future. Robot probes have already discovered sources of valuable minerals which lie on planets, moons and other objects. The Sun, meanwhile, could provide a virtually limitless supply of power. The only problems we face are how to tap these far-flung sources of wealth and energy.

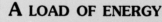

SUN POWER

Many spacecraft have used solar panels to convert sunlight into electricity (*above*). There are plans to construct huge solar panels in orbit. These would beam the power they produce down to receiving stations on Earth.

A LOAD OF ENERGY

There is thought to be a great deal of helium-3 on the Moon, bound up in deposits of titanium on the surface. Helium-3 – not found naturally on Earth – is an ideal fuel for nuclear fusion reactors. There is thought to be enough helium-3 on the Moon to supply the Earth's power needs for 700 years, assuming the problems of making a helium-3 fusion reactor can be overcome. Just one Space Shuttle load (25 tonnes – *above*) could supply the energy needs of the USA for one year, helping to light cities, such as New York, at night (*left*).

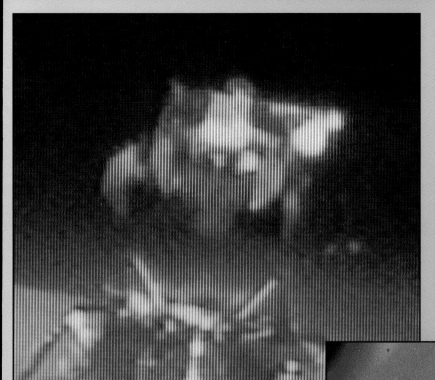

LEAVING IS EASY

Because the Moon has less gravity than the Earth, spacecraft leaving the Moon use only 5% of the energy that they would use when leaving the Earth. Apollo astronauts needed only a small rocket motor to blast clear of the Moon (*left* and *below*). Because of this, the Moon would make an ideal launch pad for missions into space, saving enormous amounts of fuel and money.

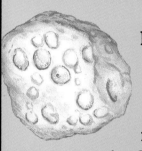

MINING THE ASTEROIDS

Although most of the asteroids, the majority of which orbit the Sun between Mars and Jupiter, are made of stone, many are part stone and metal and some are pure metal, especially iron and nickel. The asteroids range in size from small stones right up to mini-planets 1,000 km (625 miles) across. They represent a potentially enormous source of mineral wealth and in the future space ships might extract the useful materials they contain. These asteroids could be mined in the Asteroid Belt or captured and brought back to Earth orbit where they could be mined more easily.

FUTURE MISSIONS

The immediate future holds many new and exciting developments in space exploration. These include the return of a probe to Saturn, the possibility of people landing on Mars and the construction of replacements for the ageing Space Shuttle fleet.

BACK TO SATURN

Cassini (*above*) will reach Saturn in 2004 and spend four years in orbit looking at the planet. It also carries a small probe called Huygens which it will drop onto Saturn's moon, Titan.

TAKE-OFF

Like the Space Shuttle, VentureStar will blast off vertically from a launch pad (*below*) and glide down to land like a plane.

VENTURESTAR

The X-33 (*above*) is a half-sized test model of the planned VentureStar, the replacement for the Space Shuttle. This will use a new design of rocket called an aerospike and it will also be built from the latest materials which will make the VentureStar very light. This means that it will not need the rocket boosters and fuel tank used by the Shuttle, making it the first single-stage launch vehicle. As a result, a VentureStar mission should cost one tenth that of a Space Shuttle flight.

NEAR to Eros

The Near Earth Asteroid Rendezvous, or NEAR, was launched in February 1996. It is due to arrive in orbit around the asteroid called 433 Eros in February 2000 (*right*). NEAR will orbit the asteroid for about a year, getting to within 24 km (15 miles) of its surface.

Journey to Mars

Using similar methods to the Apollo Moon missions, a mission to Mars would cost nearly $400 billion. However, there is a cheaper alternative. Using a programme called Mars Direct, a robot factory would be sent to the red planet first (*left*). On Mars, this robot factory would start to create fuel from the Martian atmosphere. In a year, it could make enough fuel for a return journey to Earth. A second ship could then leave for Mars, carrying a human crew (*below*) and without carrying all the fuel. This method would cut the cost of any Mars mission to just $50 billion.

VentureStar™

TO THE STARS

Today's rockets have launched many objects into space. However, conventional rockets are not powerful enough to push spacecraft across the huge distances to the stars. New forms of propulsion systems have been suggested to do this. These include ramjets and even sailing on the solar wind.

CANON POWER
Research has been carried out into firing robot probes into space using a large gun (*left*). The probes would not need rockets or fuel, making them lighter and cheaper to launch.

NUCLEAR VOYAGER
In the late 1970's, the British Interplanetary Society made plans for a two-stage fusion craft called Daedalus (*left*). This would take a trip to the nearby (in interstellar terms) Barnard's Star, about six light years away. During the 50-year trip the craft would accelerate to 12% of the speed of light. The engine would gain its power from micro-fusion explosions using appropriate fuel. The craft would scoop up this fuel from the atmosphere of Jupiter as it headed out of the Solar System.

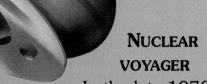

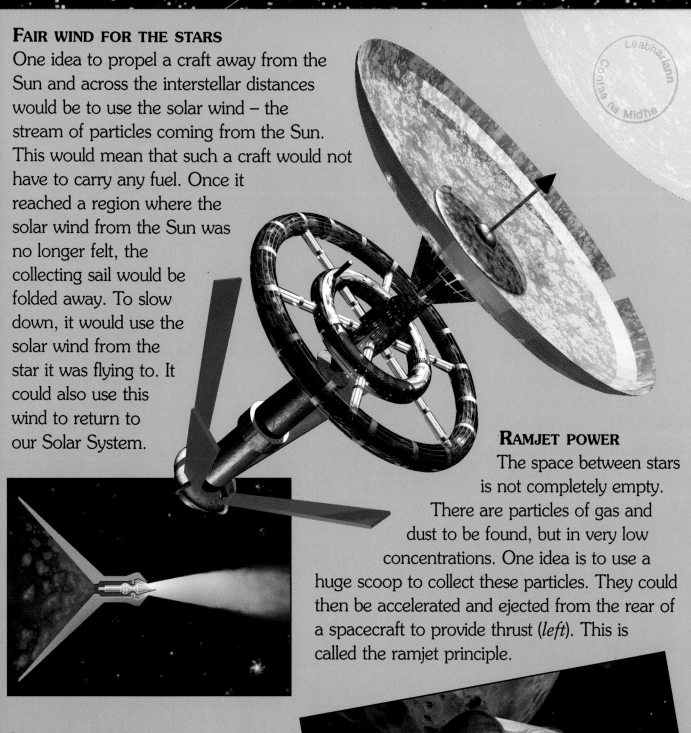

FAIR WIND FOR THE STARS

One idea to propel a craft away from the Sun and across the interstellar distances would be to use the solar wind – the stream of particles coming from the Sun. This would mean that such a craft would not have to carry any fuel. Once it reached a region where the solar wind from the Sun was no longer felt, the collecting sail would be folded away. To slow down, it would use the solar wind from the star it was flying to. It could also use this wind to return to our Solar System.

RAMJET POWER

The space between stars is not completely empty. There are particles of gas and dust to be found, but in very low concentrations. One idea is to use a huge scoop to collect these particles. They could then be accelerated and ejected from the rear of a spacecraft to provide thrust (*left*). This is called the ramjet principle.

INTO THE ARK

Even with the most advanced rockets, getting to the stars may still take tens of years. A human crew would need a sustainable food supply, maybe even growing their own crops and rearing their own animals. One idea proposed by NASA scientists would be to build an enormous space ark (*right*). This would house roughly 3,500 sq km (1,300 sq miles) of living area.

GLOSSARY

Asteroids
Small rocky objects, the greatest collection of which orbit the Sun in a large band called the Asteroid Belt. This is found between Mars and Jupiter.

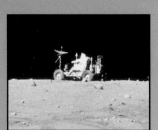

Astronauts
People who travel into space are called astronauts. Russian astronauts are known as cosmonauts.

Atmosphere
The layer of gases that surrounds a planet. The atmosphere around Earth supplies us with the oxygen we need to stay alive.

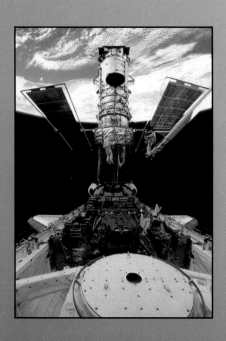

Comets
Lumps of ice and dust that orbit around the Sun. When they get near the Sun, they throw off huge amounts of gas and debris, creating tails which stream out behind them.

Electromagnetic spectrum
The entire range of radiation, ranging from radio waves to gamma rays. It also includes all the colours of visible light and the invisible forms of radiation, such as infrared light, as well as x-rays.

Gravity
Every object in the Universe has a force which attracts it to every other object. This force is called gravity. The more dense the object, the greater its gravitational force. A large and very dense object, such as the Sun, will have a higher gravitational force than a smaller, less dense object, such as the Earth.

Moons
Small bodies that orbit some of the major planets. The Earth has one moon and Jupiter has at least 16!

Nuclear fusion
The process by which atoms are squeezed together and fused under high pressures and temperatures. This process gives out enormous amounts of energy, causing stars to shine.

Observatory
A building which houses a telescope.

Orbit
The path of an object, such as a planet or a comet, around another object, such as a star.

Planets
Large objects that orbit around a star. These can be rocky planets such as the Earth, Venus and Mars, or gassy giant planets, such as Jupiter, Uranus or Saturn.

Rings
The larger, gassy planets, such as Jupiter and Saturn, are surrounded by rings. These rings are not solid as they appear from a distance, but are made up of millions of particles of rock and ice.

Rockets
Rockets are powerful motors which produce thrust by burning fuel to make gases expand. These expanding gases push on the rocket, forcing it forward.

Satellite
An object that goes around, or orbits, another, larger object. Satellites can be natural, such as moons, or artificial, such as weather satellites.

Solar panels
Thin, wafer-like structures which can convert sunlight into electricity to power a spacecraft.

Solar System
The group of major planets, including the Earth, minor planets, moons and comets that orbit the Sun.

Solar wind
A stream of charged particles thrown off by the Sun.

Stages
Rockets may come in parts, called stages. Each stage contains its own rocket motors and fuel tanks.

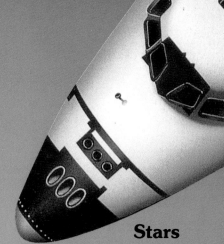

Stars
Objects which make huge amounts of heat and light. They do this by squashing together the gas particles which make them up, in a process called nuclear fusion.

Telescopes
Devices that magnify (make bigger) an object that is being looked at. Astronomers use telescopes to look at the stars and the planets. Telescopes can collect visible light, or they can catch invisible radiation, including radio waves and infrared radiation.

INDEX

Photo credits:
Abbreviations:
t-top, m-middle, b-bottom, r-right,
l-left, c-centre

All the photography in this book is
provided by NASA except the
following pages:
Cover br, 1, 5b, 9tl, 26, 29mr, 32,
34b, 34-35 & 36t – Frank Spooner
Pictures. 4t – Jon Kirkwood.
4bl – Spectrum Colour Library.
4br, 5t, 6m, 11b, 20br & 38br –
Roger Vlitos. 6b, 7 both, 8 all, 9ml
& b & 19 both – Science Photo
Library. 9tm, tr & mr – Mary Evans
Picture Library. 15t – Eye
Ubiquitous. 27t – European Space
Agency. 30b –
    Aerospatiale. 31tl –
    MGM (courtesy
    Kobal).

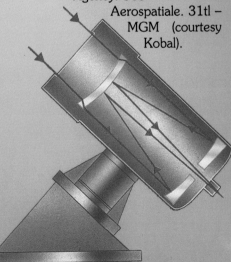